W9-AOD-407

Tribute to an Artist

The Jamestown Paintings of Sidney E. King

Tribute to an Artist

The Jamestown Paintings of Sidney E. King

James A. Crutchfield

The Dietz Press
Richmond, Virginia

© 2006 by James A. Crutchfield
All Rights Reserved
Published 2007

ISBN: 0-87517-133-8
Library of Congress Catalog Number: 2006929129

Published by The Dietz Press
Richmond, Virginia
www.dietzpress.com

Printed in Canada

To the memory of Sidney E. King
and to the people of Virginia who have benefited from his talents.

Contents

Plates

Acknowledgments

Several people, most of whom I've never met, assisted me greatly with the compilation and writing of this book. Sidney King's works are so widespread across the country that I doubt if anyone knows the location of them all, and I needed all the help I could get in tracking down the ones contained herein. As I came across a reference to one of his paintings and followed up with an inquiry, I was always met with a friendly voice on the other end of the telephone, representing a person who was genuinely interested in what I was trying to accomplish and who was eager to help.

Especially I would like to thank Mike Litterst, Public Affairs Officer at the Colonial National Historical Park in Yorktown, Virginia. A great many of the paintings reproduced in this book came from the U. S. National Park Service's collections, and Mike adroitly cut through the red tape to obtain the permissions I needed to get the project underway.

To Karam Hwang of the John D. Rockefeller, Jr. Library at the Colonial Williamsburg Foundation; to Roberta Hair Grainger of the Jamestown-Yorktown Foundation; and to Catherine E. Dean of APVA Preservation Virginia go my deep appreciation for their assistance in locating King paintings in their collections and allowing them to be reproduced.

I had many conversations with Mike Kelly, Director of Communications for the Intermet Corporation of Troy, Michigan. In my preliminary research, I discovered that in 1983, Intermet had acquired Lynchburg Foundry Company, and with it, two of King's large oil paintings, although they depicted non-Jamestown scenes. Over the years, Lynchburg Foundry's in-house magazine, *The Iron Worker,* had also carried feature stories about King and his art in at least three issues and I am indebted to Mike for allowing me to use several of the photographs from the articles.

Craig Schulin of *The Free Lance-Star*, the local newspaper in Fredericksburg, Virginia, discovered a wealth of information about Sidney King, the man and the artist, from the large number of news and feature items that had run in his paper over the years. Thanks to Craig for sending these clippings. The folks at the *Richmond Times-Dispatch* also helped in my data gathering by sharing their news files.

Fred Anderson, executive director of the Virginia Baptist Historical Society, was well acquainted with Sidney King and kindly sent several news and periodical clippings and shared with me his many conversations with the artist.

Paul Keeler of Caroline County, Virginia, King's stepson, read the manuscript and his suggestions have, no doubt, made the book better than it would have been without his review.

Of course, this project would never have been possible without the encouragement and support of the publisher, The Dietz Press. Both Wert Smith and Robert Dietz realized early on the significance of the Jamestown 400th Anniversary event in 2007 and wanted to produce a quality memento for the occasion. I believe they have accomplished their goal with this book.

Introduction

The old saying goes, "A picture is worth a thousand words," and that was the intent when, more than half a century ago, the National Park Service commissioned Sidney King to create a series of epic oil paintings depicting the history of Jamestown.

For many people, including writer James A. Crutchfield, King's art captured notable events that had occurred in Jamestown's past in a way that sparked a lifelong interest in the region's history – and in the artist who had so aptly portrayed it. Sidney King's perspective and talent brought to life the people who, in 1607, settled the tiny island that became the genesis of Virginia. The paintings scattered across the landscape gave shape, form, and dimension more fully than the words that accompanied the paintings.

To say that Sidney King was driven as an artist may be an understatement. Continuing to paint long after retirement and almost to the day he died, he viewed painting not simply as a means to make a living or as an avenue to gain fame, but also to satisfy an undeniable need. King was practical about his art. This was his profession. Rather than choose to paint for a popular market or to work through dealers and galleries, he elected to focus his interest on history and soon found his market through interpreting historic sites. Interest, talent, and timing conspired to be advantageous. At the time, Americans were on the brink of notable anniversaries related to Jamestown, the Revolution, and the Civil War. A patriotic spirit pervaded the public, spurring an interest in historic sites and the stories they had to tell.

Travel and media also helped set the stage. The ever increasing popularity of the automobile created a surge in family travel following World War II. The wonder of television soon entered the mainstream. TV series such as Walter Cronkite's *You Are There* (1953-1957) brought historic moments right into the living room, inspiring families to launch out on summer vacations to experience history where it happened.

At Jamestown, King believed himself to be a journalist, documenting the accounts of the seventeenth century in order to give visitors the opportunity to understand the events that had occurred there. Most of his paintings, even those whose primary purpose was to document a structure, contain images of people engaged in activities – a woman carrying a basket in front of the Third and Fourth statehouse, or an aerial view of the fort revealing settlers pursuing their trades. People relate to people and then they relate to the events, a natural progression that King exploited time and time again. Thus, by humanizing the subject matter, he achieved his main goal of teaching history.

"[My] primary purpose is historical accuracy in pictures that tell the story of the past in an interesting manner," King once wrote. He worked with National Park Service professionals, including archaeologist John Cotter and Jamestown Museum curator J. Paul Hudson to ensure the accuracy of his paintings. Recent discoveries at Jamestown reveal how the colonists built the structures, the types of weapons they carried, and the kinds of industry they attempted. King highlighted the major events – the Starving Times, the Indian uprising in 1622, and the first legislative assembly. He also documented life. He did all this within the context of what was known in the 1950s about life at Jamestown.

On the eve of the four hundredth anniversary of the founding at Jamestown, it is instructive to look back at the work of Sidney King and to appreciate how it helped shape our understanding of early Virginia. The ongoing work of APVA Preservation Virginia's archaeological team at Historic Jamestowne is rewriting many of the assumptions of earlier historians. Archeological evidence proves that more than eighty-five percent of the 1607 fort remains intact on the banks of the James River. The site selected for the fort is no longer considered to have been ill-suited for settlement, but rather that it represented the Virginia Company's orders for choosing a location that was defensible to ward off the much-feared Spanish foe.

A more fully developed understanding of the aims of the first settlers has also been gained. The colonizing expedition was an entrepreneurial venture and paved the way for the American spirit of financial success that we hold dear. The men who arrived in 1607 found commodities to export – gold, timber, raw materials for glass – thus allowing repayment to the Virginia Company investors. The recovery of more than one million artifacts from the site of James Fort bears witness to the preparedness of the colonists. Crucibles for assaying gold and for refining glass, agricultural and trade tools, medical instruments, and jars for stores reveal a wealth of materials. Trade beads, bits of rolled copper, and fragments of Virginia Indian-made pottery support the fact that the neighboring Powhatan Indians maintained a well-developed society and that the intent of the colonists was to establish a trading relationship with them for sustenance rather than to grow their own crops. A drought, the worst in seven hundred years as evidenced by tree ring studies, uncovers the reason that this trade relationship was less than successful. The ecosystem was under stress. Food was scarce, the water sources were affected, and tensions ensued.

Though Sidney King was not privy to these new findings, his visions of a seventeenth-century world in Virginia appear in countless textbooks offering an artistic snapshot, a starting point that inspires a new generation just learning about history. Our understanding of the historic record will continue to be enhanced by research and study. James A. Crutchfield's book positions King's paintings once again as a starting point – artistic renderings that capture the imagination of the moment, inspiring us to turn to the site of these events and to find out what happened next.

Elizabeth S. Kostelny
Executive Director
APVA Preservation Virginia

"I've found an artist needs discipline.
I've learned to regiment my moods —
re-create mood from the subject
and not wait for a bolt from the blue as inspiration."

— Sidney E. King, 1956.

A Word to the Reader

This book is a memorial to an artist I never knew. I became acquainted with his work almost forty years ago when I first toured Jamestown, Virginia, and took the one-way loop automobile drive around the Island. I was most impressed with this man's panoramic paintings, placed at strategic locations along the route and depicting places, events, and handicrafts associated with the early history of England's first permanent colony in North America. At the time of my visit, the 350th anniversary of Jamestown's settlement, celebrated in 1957, was not too far in the past. The Visitor Center bookstore still stocked a few publications commemorating the event, one of which was a paperbound album of the artist's works, printed in black and white – the ones I had just experienced on the loop-drive and which I soon learned had been commissioned by the National Park Service for the occasion. I eagerly purchased a copy and still have it.

The artist's name was Sidney E. King and, over the years as I revisited Jamestown and environs time and again, I always re-drove the one-way loop to admire his paintings. On each occasion, they thrilled me as if I had never seen them before, and, each time, the musings and events of the present-day disappeared as I observed the paintings and, then, in my mind, interpreted the landscape before me into images conjuring up scenes from nearly four centuries ago.

Tribute to an Artist

Sidney Eugene King was born in Boston – more precisely, Dorchester – Massachusetts, on August 22, 1906, just four months after the legendary earthquake destroyed San Francisco, killing seven hundred in its wake and unleashing a savage fury that racked up nearly one-half billion dollars worth of damages. It was a time when Theodore Roosevelt was president of the United States and the country was beginning to flex its muscles on the international scene. That year, the Pure Food and Drug Act was enacted by Congress, along with the federal Meat Inspection Act, both devised to render increased protection to the consumer. Charles Evans Hughes – who one day would become Chief Justice of the U. S. Supreme Court and the Republican candidate for president – defeated newspaper mogul William Randolph Hearst for the governorship of New York. And, in New Jersey, Princeton University president Woodrow Wilson, who six years later would be elected president of the United States, declared that the automobile was "a picture of the arrogance of wealth, with all its independence and carelessness."

In other events of this momentous year, President Roosevelt became the first American to win the Nobel Peace Prize for his work in terminating the Russo-Japanese War of the previous year. Denmark's King Christian IX died and India's Mohandas K. Gandhi inaugurated his world-wide campaign of non-violent resistance against racial discrimination. The Chicago White Sox defeated the Chicago Cubs in the World Series. Prominent New York architect Stanford White was gunned

Sidney Eugene King

During his eight decades of painting, Sidney Eugene King (1906 – 2002) carried the art of the mural to new heights, creating at the age of sixty, what is believed to be the largest such in North America. The monumental painting, located in Salt Lake City, measures four hundred feet long by seventy-five feet high and depicts the history of the Church of Jesus Christ of Latter Day Saints.

Photograph is reproduced from The Iron Worker, *courtesy of the Intermet Corporation.*

down by Pittsburgh millionaire Harry K. Thaw, whose wife, the infamous "girl in the red velvet swing" was once White's mistress. And, out in Texas, the King Ranch acquired sufficient acreage to push its holdings over the one million acre mark.

⌗ ⌗ ⌗ ⌗

Even as a young child, King was always fascinated by art. While studying at the Museum School of Fine Arts in Boston, he came under the tutelage of John Singer Sargent (1856-1925), the American portraitist who in later life carved out a new career as an impressionist water colorist and muralist. In fact, Sargent had been commissioned by the Museum to produce the murals that beautify the Rotunda today. No doubt, as King observed his mentor at work, he was awed by the elder artist's deftness at creating larger than life paintings. In later life, King noted that "John Singer Sargent was a master of mural painting," adding that, "He was a guidepost for me and my work and after studying under him, I really set my sights on mural painting."

Following additional training at the Massachusetts Normal School of Practical Art, the Vesper George School of Art, and the Scott Carvey School of Art, King opened his own studio in Boston. His carpenter father pleaded with him to get a real job, but art was in young King's blood and he was determined to find ways to express himself. Like so many fine painters before and since, his first pursuit was commercial design and, during this phase of his early career, he provided scores of illustrations for such magazines as *Open Road for Boys.* He also produced artistic material for travel agencies and designed labels for commercial canned goods.

When his partner in the Boston studio died in 1929, and with the financial woes of the Great Depression closing in and making it harder to make ends meet, King's artistic visions changed course. He liquidated his company, purchased a Model T Ford and decided to "see the country and record it in watercolor." He traveled all over the United States for the next year and a half. Later taking a job with an organization that sponsored educational tours of the South for children, he was in Fredericksburg, Virginia in 1939, when the company ceased operations. By then, his personal limited funds were exhausted as well, so he gave up his vagabond adventuring and decided to find more gainful employment.

⌗ ⌗ ⌗ ⌗

During World War II, while working at the military base at Quantico, Virginia, King painted this nine feet high by fourteen feet long mural commemorating U. S. Marines raising the American flag on Iwo Jima. Painting is reproduced from *The Iron Worker*, courtesy of the Intermet Corporation.

King loved the Fredericksburg area and, years later, related that "I really had a hunch that my future lay in this part of the country," emphasizing that "I liked Virginia, so I decided to settle here." Rescued by a Salvation Army captain who found temporary work for him, King, along with a new partner, soon opened a sign-painting shop in Fredericksburg. He was approached by representatives of the National Park Service who commissioned him to create narrative signage for several of the federal battlefield park properties in the area. His artistic temperament rebelled at the idea of painting words. "I detested the work for it was so monotonous and beside[s] . . . . I wanted to see paintings, depicting what actually happened at the sites, erected in the place of the narrative panels," he once told a newspaper reporter from the *Rappahannock Times*.

A big break occurred for King during those early struggling years, when, in 1942, he received a commission by Russell Walther, the manager of Oak Hill Stables near Fredericksburg. The stables' owner, A. W. Mitchell, had originally hired King to paint billboards along State Highway 3 which ran near his property. When the artist was approached by Walther and asked if he thought he could paint a few fox hunting scenes on the walls of the stables, he jumped at the chance. Substituting for models were Mary Washington College students, many of whom frequented the stables and were expert riders. When the great flood of October, 1942 – an incident King described as "one great big event I'll never forget" – flooded the rivers and streams of the region, he assisted the young Mary Washington women with rescuing stranded residents along Highway 3.

It was while living in Fredericksburg that King discovered another love, his first wife, the former Peggy Taylor. Following a two-year courtship, the couple married and settled in Peggy's ancestral home located southeast of Bowling Green. The one hundred acre farm was part of an original plantation of 3,700 acres granted to early Caroline County settler, John Taylor, one of Peggy's ancestors. Mrs. King soon became an able assistant to the artist, "handling all of the grindwork, such as the buying of materials, shipping, and handling of contacts and correspondence."

⌘ ⌘ ⌘ ⌘

During World War II, King worked at the Quantico Marine base outside Washington, D. C., where he designed insignia for military aircraft, created "incentive" posters to help boost the Marine Corps recruiting program, and actually painted camouflage on the airplanes with a spray gun. When his work there was done, he left behind on an aircraft hangar wall one of his most enduring paintings, a rendition of victorious U. S.

Marines raising the American flag atop Mount Suribachi on Iwo Jima on February 23, 1945. The painting, based on the famous photograph by Joe Rosenthal, is fourteen feet long by nine feet high and was created, not using normal artist's materials, but with a common paint spray-gun and conventional paint.

Following the war, King returned to Fredericksburg and resumed his sign painting. Before long, he found himself again working with the U. S. National Park Service creating the narrative panels that explained various battle scenes in the several military parks dotting the central Virginia region. He also began painting outdoor panoramas of the narrated events which were well received by park officials.

He realized that the forces of Nature would quickly cause his murals to deteriorate. As a result, he worked closely with the E. I. Du Pont Company and chemists, including his own brother-in-law, to develop pigments that would withstand the sun's ultraviolet rays, the intense humidity, and the extreme temperature fluctuations to which the paintings would be exposed. Cooperating with the Rohm-Haas Company, he helped design the waterproof, airtight, plexiglas display cases that housed the murals.

King's reputation for providing quality, accurate work impressed the Park Service management and, in the mid-1950s, as plans were being laid for the upcoming 350th anniversary of the English settlement at Jamestown, he was commissioned to paint a large number of outdoor murals to be placed at various historical sites on Jamestown Island.

When King was commissioned by the U. S. National Park Service to produce a series of paintings that would depict everyday life in Jamestown, he assembled a team of professionals whose technical advice assured that his renditions would be as historically accurate as possible. Shown here (left to right) are King, Architect A. Lawrence Kocher, Archaeologist John L. Cotter, and Jamestown Museum Curator J. Paul Hudson. Photograph is reproduced from *The Iron Worker*, courtesy of the Intermet Corporation.

The project would take several years to complete and to insure accuracy in his paintings, King worked closely with Park officials and other professionals, especially J. Paul Hudson, curator of the Jamestown Museum; historical architects A. Lawrence Kocher and Charles C. Forman; archaeologists J. C. Harrington, Edward B. Jelks, and Dr. John L. Cotter; and historian Charles E. Hatch, Jr. He scoured libraries and archival sources all over the eastern United States to expand his knowledge of the times that he would graphically document. He also traveled to England to observe, first-hand, late Medieval architecture, artifacts, and material culture so that he would possess a firm foundation of knowledge of the Jamestown settlement period.

In 1957, the National Park Service published its book, *New Discoveries at Jamestown,* written by King's associates, John L. Cotter and J. Paul Hudson. It provided a comprehensive overview of the early history and archaeology of the colony and, although not stated on the title page, contained nearly forty detailed images created by King that depicted everything from the cross-section of an early water well to a family dining scene. In 1963, King and Hudson released their *A Pictorial Album of Jamestown,* which contained black and white reproductions of many of the artist's paintings that he had created for the Jamestown 350th anniversary celebration, specially designed copies of which had earlier been presented to President Dwight Eisenhower and Queen Elizabeth II when they toured the Island. He received grateful acknowledgment from both leaders.

The Jamestown project was the beginning of a long-term relationship between King and the National Park Service. Over the next few years, he produced nearly two hundred historical murals, most of them measuring four by eight feet, for federally operated parks all over the eastern United States, including those at Jamestown, Yorktown, Gettysburg, Manassas, Fredericksburg and Spotsylvania, Petersburg, and Kennesaw Mountain, among others. His distinctive paintings "capture[d] a feel that has become classically Park Service," a park historian once commented. In addition to the national park-commissioned works, King kept busy during these productive years painting hundreds of other historical works that ended up in private collections.

⌗ ⌗ ⌗ ⌗

If a subject existed that held the interest of Sidney King as much as American historical themes, it was religion. He had painted religious murals in local church buildings for years, but following his time with the National Park Service, the life-long Baptist artist immersed himself in a series of monumental religious paintings that eventually resulted in the largest mural ever to be painted in the United States.

This pen and ink work depicts an early frame house at Jamestown. Drawing from *New Discoveries at Jamestown,* courtesy of the U. S. National Park Service.

Sidney King's talents went far beyond his precision as an oil painter and water colorist. He was also a master with pen and ink as evidenced by this fine, detailed drawing of an eighteenth century ship loading pig iron from a Virginia wharf. Drawing is reproduced from *The Iron Worker,* courtesy of the Intermet Corporation.

The first of these, completed in 1964, was a 110 feet long by eight and one-half feet high painting that depicted in twelve panels the life and times of Jesus Christ. The huge mural, commissioned by the Church of Jesus Christ of Latter Day Saints and displayed in the Mormon Pavilion at the New York World Fair in 1964, was viewed by tens of thousands of onlookers. "There is no doubt in my mind," King related at the time, "that this is the most important thing I have ever attempted," adding that "I'm putting everything I've got into it." The individual paintings comprising the mural represented scenes from Christ's life from his baptism in the Jordan River through the Crucifixion and Resurrection.

His next big commission dwarfed even the World's Fair project. Again, officials of the Mormon Church, so satisfied with "The Life of Christ," hired King to decorate the dome of their new Information Center in Salt Lake City and to produce a four hundred feet long by seventy-five feet high mural to cover the supporting walls encircling the dome. The resulting work is called "Creation" and, according to King, "represents the Master's grand scheme symbolized in planetary formations." The night sky in the dome is portrayed exactly as it was on the night of April 6, 1830, the date from which the Church claims its origins. King reported that several hundred gallons of paint were required to complete the project and that he had the assistance of two hundred workmen to hang the canvases. Even more spectacular than the "The Life of Christ," the "Creation" project was claimed by the artist to be his best work ever and, at the time, was the country's largest painting.

King's last large mural project was completed for the Virginia Baptist Historical Society at its headquarters on the campus of the University of Richmond. Produced between 1985 and 1990, the painting consists of thirty-five separate panels and depicts significant events and personages throughout Virginia Baptist history.

❈ ❈ ❈ ❈

Sidney King thrived on work. Whether he was creating a portrait of a relative, a landscape for a friend, or a commissioned piece for a church, museum, or railroad station, he produced paintings at a prodigious rate, sometimes turning out one per week. He received requests for paintings from individuals and institutions all over the United States and exhibited in a number of museums, including the American Historical Museum in Chadd's Ford, Pennsylvania; the Maritime Museum of Philadelphia; and the Museum of Natural History at Wilmington, Delaware. And, in the midst of all of this frantic activity, he still found time to conduct formalized art classes for more than forty years.

The list of King commissions is practically endless and includes major oils done for the Lynchburg Foundry, one of which portrays a young George Washington, accompanied by his father, Augustine, peering into the white hot fires of one of the elder Washington's iron furnaces. Another depicts the March, 1622, Indian raid on the Falling Creek Iron Works near Richmond. One of his hunting scenes once graced the walls of the Holiday Inn in Fredericksburg and a local truck stop displayed a forty feet by eighty feet mural depicting the history of transportation. An epic mural to be displayed in the lobby of the Union Bank and Trust Company in Bowling Green, Virginia, was commissioned by the bank in 1973 and required seven and one-half months for King to complete. Measuring seventy-one feet long by eight feet tall, the huge painting depicts nineteen separate scenes taken from Caroline County history.

When King was not busy with commissioned work, he created paintings just for their beauty. A brochure that

Two Jamestown housewives brew homemade beer in this conjectural pen and ink sketch. Drawing from *New Discoveries at Jamestown*, courtesy of the U. S. National Park Service.

accompanied one of his exhibits in Bowling Green, Virginia, in early March, 1970 listed such nostalgic titles as "Woodland Azaleas," "Winter Landscape in Glacier Park," "The Relentless Sea," and "Fishermen on the Chesapeake." Others bore titles of "Fox Hounds, "Children at Play," and "Hawaiian Sunset." In performing research for this book, the author talked to many individuals who were proud owners of non-historical King paintings. The versatile artist obviously enjoyed expressing himself in a variety of genres.

His vision was limitless. "Though I try to be exact in my murals," he once explained, "I'm not really of the photographic school because at the time of the scenes I create there were no cameras," adding emphatically that, "There must be some imagination."

But King was more than a master with oils, acrylics, and water colors. He also was a precision pen and ink artist and his wares have illustrated many books on subjects ranging from the biography of Colonel John Pelham, the youthful Confederate artilleryman assigned to General J. E. B. Stuart's cavalry, to a history of George Washington's Ferry Farm near Fredericksburg, to the archaeology of Jamestown. His sometimes rapidly made drawings show a keen knowledge of subject matter and served the artist as preliminary sketches for more complex oil or water color pieces. "I've done every subject under the sun," King once observed, "I get tired of one subject and go on to another."

King's overall attitude toward art can readily be summed up in a simple, oft-quoted statement: "It's a colorful country of ours, and I've made it my business to make sure Mr. and Mrs. America get a glimpse of things as they happened."

⊠ ⊠ ⊠ ⊠

When Sidney King died on April 24, 2002, at the age of ninety-five, at his home, "The Willows," in Caroline County, he had painted for nearly eighty years –sometimes eight hours a day, six days a week. Today, it is almost unfathomable to imagine the total number of drawings, paintings, and murals that he created over his lifetime. Although he might have slowed his pace somewhat – but not much – during his later years, the idea of giving up painting altogether never occurred to him. "Retiring doesn't sound good to me at all" he declared at age ninety-one, "If I quit, I fall apart."

Although he was content to be able to earn a living doing what he liked to do best, the idea of making money for money's sake never occurred to him. "The pleasure I have is turning out something that someone else will enjoy," he once confided to a reporter, and among his greatest pleasures were the bi-annual sales he held in his studio, wherein people flocked to purchase a Sidney King original, sometimes for mere dollars each.

Over the years, as King's reputation and popularity climbed, National Park Service officials finally realized that his commissioned works at the various Park sites were more than just mere illustrations – indeed, they were fine art. His Jamestown paintings and others placed throughout the Park system are presently being removed from their original locations and taken indoors for protection from the elements. As the hundreds and thousands of artifacts that vie with each other for public display within visitor centers continue to increase and be interpreted, many of them fail to see the light of day. It is hoped that Sidney King's outstanding depictions of the life and times of early Jamestown will always find a prominent place for viewing by successive generations of visitors to England's first permanent settlement in North America.

This intricate black and white study portrays the maddening activity that occurred
on the Jamestown wharf whenever a ship arrived from England.
Drawing from *New Discoveries at Jamestown,* courtesy of the U. S. National Park Service.

The Plates

Everyday Life at Jamestown

"[My] primary purpose is historical accuracy
in pictures that tell the story of the past
in an interesting manner. Art may be there,
but it is coincidental."

— Sidney E. King, 1956

The Landfall

"The first land they made they called Cape Henry, where anchoring,
Mr. Wingfield, Gosnoll, and Newport, with 30 others,
recreating themselves on shore, were assaulted by 5 savages,
who hurt 2 of the English very dangerously."

John Smith

⊠ ⊠ ⊠ ⊠

Although the story of Jamestown and the first permanent English settlement in North America originated in 1584, when Englishmen accompanying the first of Sir Walter Raleigh's three ill-fated trans-Atlantic expeditions observed the wonders of North America along the present-day North Carolina coast, the colony's real beginnings date to 1607. During the previous year, King James I presented a group of English entrepreneurs with a charter to organize the Virginia Company of London with authority to exploit, colonize, and administer the vast region known as Virginia. In December, three galleons – the *Susan Constant, Discovery,* and *Godspeed* – slipped their moorings near London and drifted down the Thames River, soon to be engulfed by the mighty Atlantic Ocean. During late April, 1607, after an eighteen-week-long voyage, the small fleet, commanded by Captain Christopher Newport, sighted Cape Henry at the mouth of the Chesapeake Bay.

Captain John Smith, who was one of seven counselors named to govern the colony, described the site of the first landfall in his book, *A Map of Virginia,* published in 1612. "There is but one entrance by sea into this country," he wrote, "and that is at the mouth of a very goodly Bay the width whereof is near 18 or 20 miles." Continuing, he reported that:

> The cape on the Southside is called Cape Henry in honor of our most noble Prince. The show of the land there is a white hilly sand like unto the Downes, and along the shores great plenty of pines and firs . . . . Within is a country that may have the prerogative over the most pleasant places of Europe, Asia, Africa, or America, for large and pleasant navigable rivers, heaven & earth never agreed better to frame a place for man's habitation being of our constitutions, were it fully manured and inhabited by industrious people. Here are mountains, hills, plains, valleys, rivers, and brooks, all running most pleasantly into a fair bay . . . with fruitful and delightful land.

Landing of the First Settlers at Cape Henry, April 1607
Courtesy of the National Park Service, Colonial National Historical Park, Jamestown Collection.

Going Ashore on Jamestown Island

*"The thirteenth day, we came to our seating place . . .
where our ships do lie so near the shore that they
are moored to the trees in six fathom water."*

George Percy

❈ ❈ ❈ ❈

For two weeks following the first sighting of Cape Henry, Captain Newport and his adventurers explored the numerous streams, inlets, and marshes along the Atlantic coast. Proceeding up one of the waterways – a broad river that dumped its waters into the Chesapeake Bay and later was named the James in honor of the king – the three ships, crew, and passengers eventually moored near a spit of favorable-looking land situated near the north bank. The date was May 14, 1607, and the site selected for settlement was present-day Jamestown Island.

The list of 105 new arrivals included four carpenters, two bricklayers, one blacksmith, one mason, one tailor, one preacher, one drummer, one barber, one "sailer," and two surgeons. Twelve others were listed as laborers and the rest were classified as either members of the Council, gentlemen, or boys. The amount of work that awaited so few skilled craftsmen was awesome, but according to John Smith, everyone pitched in. "The Council contrived [designed] the fort," he wrote, and "the rest cut down trees to make place to pitch their tents; some provide clapboard . . . some make gardens, some nets, etc." Smith also revealed that despite the workers' every activity being observed by neighboring curious Indians, "overwhelming jealousies" among the new colony's leadership prohibited the formation of an army for defense or the construction of a fort, other than a poorly conceived one hastily built from "boughs of trees cast together in the form of a half moon."

Settling the new colony would not be easy for the Jamestown adventurers. Not only was the site ill-suited for European habitation due to intense humidity, hoards of biting insects, and poorly drained terrain, but also food supplies were either quickly depleted or ruined due to spoilage from the fierce heat. By four months' time into the audacious colonization scheme, fifty of the newcomers had died from starvation and/or disease. "Within ten days [of the original landfall on Jamestown Island], scarce ten amongst us could either go, or well stand, such extreme weakness and sickness oppressed us," wrote a dejected John Smith several years later. But, this was only the beginning. In the years to come, conditions would continue to worsen.

Colonists Landing at Jamestown, May 14, 1607

Courtesy of the National Park Service, Colonial National Historical Park, Jamestown Collection.

Jamestown's Original Inhabitants

"The people differ very much in stature, especially in language . . .
some being very great . . . others very little . . .
but generally tall and straight, of a comely proportion,
& of a colour brown when they are of any age . . . ."

John Smith

⊞ ⊞ ⊞ ⊞

No doubt, scores of pairs of curious eyes peered at the one hundred plus Englishmen who happily disembarked from their three ships onto Jamestown Island that long ago day in May, 1607. The region was controlled by Algonquian-speaking Powhatan Indians, whose population of around nine thousand was organized into thirty distinct sub-tribes and scattered throughout more than one hundred towns and villages in present-day tidewater Virginia. The supreme authority of this loosely controlled confederation was a chief named Wahunsonacock, or, as the new arrivals would call him, Powhatan.

John Smith, in *A Map of Virginia,* left a detailed account of the Powhatan tribe which included an essay on the lifestyles and living arrangements of its people, as well as a vivid first-hand description of the great chief, Powhatan, and his entourage:

> He is . . . a tall well proportioned man, with a sour look, his head somewhat gray, his beard so thin that it seems none at all, his age near 60; of a very able and hardy body to endure any labour. About his person ordinarily attends a guard of 40 or 50 of the tallest men his country affords. Every night upon the 4 quarters of his house are 4 sentinels each standing a flight shoot from the other, and at every half hour one from the corps du guard doth hollow, unto whom every sentinel doth answer round from his stand; if any fail, they presently send forth an officer that beats him extremely.

Smith estimated that around 5,000 natives lived within sixty miles of Jamestown, but guessed that only about 1,500 qualified as warriors "fit for their wars." This was, no doubt, sobering news and the colonists must have been relieved when initial visitations by the natives turned out to be friendly. The relationship between the two peoples would not always remain peaceful, however, as the weeks, months, and years ahead sadly proved for both parties.

Outside the James Fort: Indians Watch
Courtesy of the National Park Service, Colonial National Historical Park, Jamestown Collection.

Early Industry

"Within less than seven weeks [of landfall on Jamestown Island] . . . we have sent you a taste of clapboard . . . ."

The Council of Virginia

❖ ❖ ❖ ❖

Scattered throughout John Smith's recollections of his experiences in early Jamestown, as well as in correspondence to England by various members of the Council, are numerous references to the manufacture of clapboards. In the absence of gold, silver, and jewels to bedazzle Virginia Company officials back home, the colonial leadership appears to have been trying to find any commodity of value that could be exported and therefore, fatten the Company's coffers.

Clapboards were such a commodity. They and wainscoting were both used in the building trades at a time when the primary material utilized in houses was timber. According to Edwin Tunis, a twentieth century authority on early American industry and trade, clapboards of the time were only about four feet in length and were cut out of a stump the same length using a tool called the froe. The process was called "riving."

The sharp, bottom edge of the froe was placed on the cross-sectional part of an upright log, cut to the length desired for the clapboard. After choosing the thickness of the board to be rived, the froe was repeatedly struck with a mallet, with every hit driving the metal instrument deeper into the wood. When the froe came through to the other end, the board split away from the log. When used in building and overlapping one another, precision-cut clapboards provided protection from rain.

Among the 105 original settlers of Jamestown were four carpenters: William Laxon, Edward Pising, Thomas Emry, and Robert Small. Most likely, they supervised the beginning of the clapboard industry in America, but probably garnered the support of the twelve laborers who accompanied them, as well as anyone else who could be recruited to fell timber and assist in the work. "No sooner were we landed, but the president dispersed . . . . 30 of us . . . to learn to make clapboard, cut down trees, and lay in wood," wrote John Smith. Ofttimes, the physical labor of such hard work got the best of some of the gentlemen who had been recruited to help, causing Smith to declare, ". . . the axes so often blistered their tender fingers, that commonly every third blow had a loud oath to drown the echo. . . ."

Lumber and Wood Production
Courtesy of the National Park Service, Colonial National Historical Park, Jamestown Collection.

Taking a Trip up the James River

". . .Captain Newport and my self with divers others, to the number of twenty two persons, set forward to discover the river, some fifty or sixty miles, finding it in some places broader, & in some narrower . . . ."

John Smith

⧈ ⧈ ⧈ ⧈

According to John Smith, for the first few days after the colonists' arrival on Jamestown Island, the natives "often visited us kindly." Believing that all was well, he, along with Captain Newport and twenty others set out to ascend the James River with the goal of exploring its headwaters. They passed several Indian villages on their journey and in each locale, they were treated with the utmost courtesy and respect by the natives. They found a pleasant countryside "with many fresh springs" and "the people in all places kindly entreating us, dancing and feasting us with strawberries, mulberries, bread, fish, and other [of] their country's provisions whereof we had plenty."

In exchange for the natives' hospitality, the Englishmen bestowed upon their new friends "bells, pins, needles, beads, or glasses, which so contented them that his [Captain Newport's] liberality made them follow us from place to place and ever kindly to respect us," wrote Smith. Several Indians even offered themselves as guides to assist the exploring party in its quest up the river.

After a few days, Smith and his men arrived at a town called Powhatan, the birthplace of its renowned namesake, Chief Powhatan. The place was positioned about one mile downstream from the fall line, the farthest navigable point on the river, beyond which "by reason of the rocks . . . there is not passage for a small boat." The following day, they erected a cross near the river's falls and bestowed a gown and a hatchet upon their faithful guide, before departing downriver amid "many signs of love."

Smith found the village of Powhatan, located near present-day Richmond, to be "very pleasant and strong by nature," and reported the presence of "12 houses pleasantly seated on a hill." The Englishmen visited several other villages in the region, in one of which the natives "shewed us the manner of their diving for mussels, in which they find pearls." In one of the last towns they visited, the inhabitants "seemed kindly . . . yet we perceive[d] many signs of a more jealousy in them than before." A sense of apprehension befell the adventurers.

Trading with the Indians, 1607
Courtesy of the National Park Service, Colonial National Historical Park, Jamestown Collection.

Strengthening Fortifications

*"Hereupon the President was contented the fort should be palisaded,
the ordnance mounted, his men armed and exercised, for many were
the assaults, and ambushes of the savages, and our men by their
disorderly straggling were often hurt, when the savages,
by the nimbleness of their heels, well escaped."*

John Smith

▨ ▨ ▨ ▨

Captain Smith's upriver exploring foray had been a pleasant one until, on the trip home and about twenty miles from Jamestown, the Indians suddenly became hostile. Hastening as rapidly as they could to the protection of the fort, the party discovered that the natives – four hundred of them, according to Smith's account – had already raided the post, killed a young boy, and wounded seventeen men. "Had it not chanced [that] a cross bar shot from the ships struck down a bough from a tree among them [the Indians] that caused them to retire, our men [would have] all been slain, being securely all at work and their arms in dry fat." The mention to the arms being in "dry fat" refers to the fact that none of the colony's weaponry had been unpacked from the containers in which they had made their overseas journey. This lack of accessible weapons, added to the fact that the initial fortification at Jamestown was merely "the boughs of trees cast together in the form of a half moon," had obviously left the colonists in an extremely precarious position.

Following this near-disaster, the colony's leadership ordered the strengthening of the fortifications and the conversion of the poorly-designed, existing fort into a structure that could withstand sustained Indian assaults if and when they should occur. It was hard work, and Smith bemoaned, "What toil we had, with so small a power to guard our workmen . . , watch all night, resist our enemies . . , cut down trees, and prepare the ground to plant our corn . . . ." By mid-June the new fort had been completed and was described by George Percy as "triangle wise, having three bulwarks at every corner like a half moon, and four or five pieces of artillery mounted in them. . . ." For the next six or seven days, the colonists were alarmed by ambushes by the natives, and at least five Englishmen were "cruelly wounded." How many of Powhatan's tribesmen were killed and disabled during the campaign, "we know not," wrote Smith, but declared that "they report three were slain and divers hurt."

Building the James Fort, May and June 1607
Courtesy of the National Park Service, Colonial National Historical Park, Jamestown Collection.

Captain Smith Seeks Trade with the Indians

*"The Indians thinking us near famished, with careless
kindness, offered us little pieces of bread & small handfuls of beans
or wheat, for a hatchet or a piece of copper."*

John Smith

❈ ❈ ❈ ❈

On June 22, 1607, Captain Newport and a shipload of crewmen left Jamestown for England where he would purchase supplies for the colony and recruit additional settlers. Although concerned about the safety of those left behind, he was encouraged the day before his departure, when one of Powhatan's chief's sent an emissary to Jamestown who "assure[d] us peace." The fort had been rebuilt, properly armed, and was in good repair, and, according to Smith, "all our men [are] in good health and comfort."

But, the blissful days would not last. Several of the colony's leaders took ill and one of them, Captain Bartholomew Gosnold, soon died. Another, Captain George Kendall, was expelled from the Council. Added to the internal political strife, the colonists found themselves faced with rapidly diminishing supplies and victuals. By September, nearly fifty men had perished and, with only about twenty days worth of food remaining, the friendly neighborhood natives came to the rescue with a "great store both of corn and bread ready made; and also there came such abundance of fowl into the rivers, as greatly refreshed our weak estates. . . ."

A few days later, Smith organized a trading party to visit the Indian town of Kecoughtan, located down the James River near the Chesapeake Bay. There, he negotiated for a large supply of corn. He described the village as "pleasantly seated upon three acres of ground, upon a plain, half [encircled] with a great bay of the great river. …" and consisting of eighteen houses. Over the next several days, Smith and his trading party visited other native towns as well and garnered scores of bushels of corn for their hungry neighbors at Jamestown.

Shortly afterwards, Smith encountered hostile Indians and was captured and carried before Opechancanough, the half-brother of Powhatan, and, later, before the great Powhatan, himself. For the most part, he was treated with kindness, was well fed, and was paraded around the region like a human trophy. He was eventually released, though most likely without the oft-cited influence of Powhatan's daughter, Pocahontas. In early January, 1608, he strode through the gate at Jamestown and was promptly arrested, convicted, and sentenced to death for the loss of two of his companions during the recent ordeal with the Indians.

John Smith Trading with the Powhatan Indians, 1607
Courtesy of the National Park Service, Colonial National Historical Park, Jamestown Collection.

Disaster Visits Jamestown

"The 7 of January, our town was almost quite burnt, with all our apparel and provision."

Edward Maria Wingfield

⊞ ⊞ ⊞ ⊞

Early January, 1608 was a busy time for Jamestown's inhabitants. Captain Smith returned following a brief captivity among Powhatan's tribesmen. The spurious charges against him with regard to his culpability in the recent deaths of his two companions – as well as his pending death penalty – were dropped. At about the same time, Captain Newport, aboard the *John and Francis* and fresh back from England with supplies and around sixty to eighty new settlers, weighed anchor in the James River alongside the fort. Five days later, shock waves reverberated throughout the town upon the discovery that the fort was ablaze.

Newport's ship had been accompanied from England by another craft, the *Phoenix,* captained by Francis Nelson, but off the coast of Virginia, "many perils of extreme storms and tempests" had sent her and her crew to the West Indies for refitting and re-supply. It finally arrived at Jamestown in mid-April with forty additional settlers and, although Captain Nelson brought with him fresh and abundant supplies, the colony's food reserves were soon taxed by the presence of more than one hundred new mouths to feed. But, among the two ships' passengers were badly needed craftsmen: another blacksmith, a gunsmith, two goldsmiths, six tailors, two apothecaries, a surgeon, a cooper, and several laborers.

With regard to the disastrous fire, Captain Smith, in his later recollections wrote that, ". . . by a mischance our fort was burned, and the most of our apparel, lodging and private provision, many of the old men diseased, and of our new for want of lodging, perished." In another reference, he declared that, ". . . the town, which being thatched with reeds the fire was so fierce as it burnt their palisades with their arms, bedding, apparel, and much private provision." Smith sadly reported that "Good Master Hunt, our preacher, lost all his library, and all that he had (but the clothes on his back) yet none other ever see him repine at his loss."

As disheartening as affairs had been – and were during late 1607 and most of 1608 –nothing could have prepared John Smith, who by now had been appointed the colony's president, and the rest of Jamestown's citizens to the terrible plight that was about to descend upon them: the horrible "starving time" of the winter of 1609-10.

The Burning of James Fort, 1608
Courtesy of the National Park Service, Colonial National Historical Park, Jamestown Collection.

The Starving Time

"[In order] to eat, many [of] our men[during] this starving time did run away unto the savages whom we never heard of after."

George Percy

▨ ▨ ▨ ▨

During the winter of 1609-10, the tiny colony of Jamestown was practically devastated by a combination of natural forces including extremely frigid weather, an onslaught of uncontrollable, communicable disease, and starvation. The horrible period has become known in history as the "starving time" and, before the spring days of 1610 brought respite, an estimated ninety per cent of the town's inhabitants had died from one cause or another. Makeshift funerals for the recently deceased were daily occurrences. A contributor to Captain John Smith's book, *The Generall Historie of Virginia, New-England, and the Summer Isles,* published in London in 1624, described the unbelievable conditions:

Though there be fish in the sea, fowl in the air, and beasts in the woods, their bounds are so large, they so wild, and we so weak and ignorant, we cannot much trouble them . . . . as for our hogs, hens, goats, sheep, horse, or what lived, our commanders, officers and savages daily consumed them, some small proportions sometimes we tasted, till all was devoured; then swords, arms, pieces, or any thing, we traded with the savages . . . that what by their cruelty, our governor's indiscretion, and the loss of our ships, of five hundred within six months . . . there remained not past sixty men, women and children, most miserable and poor creatures; and those were preserved for the most part, by roots, herbs, acorns, walnuts, berries, now and then a little fish. . . yea, even the very skins of our horses. Nay, so great was our famine, that a savage we slew, and buried, the poorer sort took him up again and ate him, and so did divers one another boiled and stewed with roots and herbs: And one amongst the rest did kill his wife, powdered [salted] her and had eaten part of her before it was known, for which he was executed, as he well deserved; now whether she was better roasted, boiled or carbonado'd [grilled], I know not, but of such a dish as powdered wife I never heard of. This was that time, which still to this day we called the starving time: it was too vile to say, and scarce to be believed, what we endured.

Burial of the Dead at Jamestown During Winter 1609-1610

Courtesy of the National Park Service, Colonial National Historical Park, Jamestown Collection.

The Starving Time II

". . . Powhatan still, as he found means, cut off their boats, [and]
denied them trade . . . ."

John Smith

⌗ ⌗ ⌗ ⌗

Disease and famine were not the only two factors that combined to make the winter of 1609-10 one of starvation and near disaster for Jamestown's residents. Relations with the neighboring Indians, under the leadership of Powhatan, were once again strained and, in addition to bloody skirmishes between the two parties, the tribesmen abruptly curtailed trading with the Englishmen for much-needed food, thereby making survival a real issue.

Food was not a problem with the Indians, however. Agricultural in nature, they grew everything they needed, or else they fished and hunted the neighboring streams and woods. In *The Generall Historie of Virginia, New-England, and the Summer Isles*, John Smith described the abundance and quality of the food supplies and dining habits of the natives who lived in the Jamestown region.

> In March and April they live much upon their fishing wires [weirs, or fish traps]; and feed on fish, turkeys, and squirrels. In May and June they plant their fields, and live most on acorns, walnuts, and fish. But to mend their diet, some disperse themselves in small companies, and live upon fish, beasts, crabs, oysters, land Tortoises, strawberries, mulberries, and such like. In June, July, and August, they feed upon the roots of *Tockwough* [green arrow arum] berries, fish, and green wheat [corn]. It is strange to see how their bodies alter with their diet, even as deer and wild beasts they seem fat and lean . . . . Powhatan . . . and some others that are provident, roast their fish and flesh upon hurdles . . . and keep it till scarce times.

Now, however, partially due to an unauthorized trading policy by Jamestown settlers that foolishly allowed weapons to be swapped with the natives for food and other supplies, the Indians were better armed than their adversaries and in a position to levy an attack at their leisure, should they desire. With these dark clouds rapidly gathering above them, Jamestown residents scurried outside the fort's palisades, scavenging any food they could while the Indian foe watched and patiently waited.

Starving Time, 1609-1610
Courtesy of the National Park Service, Colonial National Historical Park, Jamestown Collection.

Rescue!

". . . they descried the long-boat of the Lord la Ware,
for God would not have it so abandoned. . . [and he]. . .
met them with three ships exceedingly well furnished . . .
and again returned them to the abandoned James town."

Reverend William Symonds

⌘ ⌘ ⌘

A contributor to John Smith's book, relating his early experiences in Virginia, wrote that by the time the horrible "starving time" left Jamestown, only around sixty people out of nearly five hundred inhabitants had survived the malady. In May, 1610, when all appeared lost and as the few remaining residents of the town prepared for the worst, Sir Thomas Gates, the newly appointed lieutenant-governor of the infant colony, arrived with fresh supplies and 150 well-fed men. Smith's informant revealed that, ". . . when those noble knights did see our miseries (being strangers in the country) and could understand no more of the cause but by their own conjecture, of our clamors and complaints, or accusing or excusing one another, they embarked us with themselves, with the best means they could, and abandoning James Towne set sail for England."

Gates and the small remnant of Jamestown survivors left the island on the afternoon of June 7, but sailed only a short distance downriver before meeting the incoming tide. Setting out again the following morning, the small flotilla had proceeded a few miles further, when one of the crew spotted in the distance a longboat which he recognized as part of the fleet of Thomas West, third Baron De La Warr, the colony's newly appointed governor. De La Warr ordered all of Gates' followers to return at once to Jamestown.

When the governor personally reached Jamestown Island, he ". . . heard a sermon, read his commission, and entered into consultation for the good of the colony," then set to work revitalizing the disserted town. The village's population had risen dramatically with the arrival of both Gates and De La Warr and their followers within mere weeks of each other. Now, it numbered nearly five hundred souls who must have questioned their future as warfare against Powhatan and his followers at the Indian village of Kecoughtan was renewed.

Several weeks later, the colonists again attacked the Indians and, this time, the wife and children of an important chief were captured. In the aftermath, ". . . it was agreed upon to put the children to death [which] was effected by throwing them overboard and shooting out their brains in the water. . . ."

Arrival of Lord Delaware's Fleet at Jamestown, June 1610
Courtesy of the National Park Service, Colonial National Historical Park, Jamestown Collection.

The Lure of Tobacco

"The history of tobacco is the history of Jamestown and of Virginia.
No one staple or resource ever played a more significant role
in the history of any state or nation."

Melvin Herndon

▨ ▨ ▨ ▨

When Jamestown's first English colonists arrived in 1607, they observed the local natives smoking a form of tobacco that they grew in their village gardens. Although the Englishmen were familiar with the "noxious weed" – the plant was imported to the island nation around 1565 and smoking had become so commonplace by 1604 that King James had condemned the habit – the variety grown by the Indians was different. One colonist complained that the native plant was ". . . not of the best kind, it is but poor and weak, and of a biting taste." He added that "it grows not fully a yard above the ground, bearing a little yellow flower . . . the leaves are short and thick, somewhat round at the upper end . . . ."

In 1612, John Rolfe – who two years later would marry Pocahontas, the daughter of the powerful chief, Powhatan, in the newly constructed church in Jamestown – began experimenting with other types of tobacco attempting to find a blend to satisfy the tastes of all good Englishmen. Rolfe imported Spanish-grown varieties from Trinidad and South America and mixed them with the locally grown product. In time, he developed a blend that "no doubt but after a little more trial and expense in the curing thereof . . . will compare with the best in the West Indies." So successful were Rolfe's experiments that by the end of 1616, twenty-three hundred pounds of tobacco had been exported to England.

Jamestown's residents soon became so enamored by tobacco's potential as a cash crop that they began planting seedlings in every possible location – the town's lanes, open places, and yards. In 1617, Captain Samuel Argall found that ". . . the marketplace and streets and all other spare places [were] planted with tobacco . . . [and] the colony dispersed all about planting tobacco." Entire families sometimes went underfed because of the obsession with growing tobacco instead of food crops.

Rolfe's experimentations paid off quickly. When the colonists discovered that a good tobacco crop was worth up to six times more than any other agricultural commodity they could grow, tobacco culture mushroomed. During 1617, twenty thousand pounds of tobacco were shipped from Jamestown to England, followed by forty thousand pounds the next year.

Harvesting Tobacco
Courtesy of the National Park Service, Colonial National Historical Park, Jamestown Collection.

The Marriage of Pocahontas and John Rolfe

". . . Pocahontas, Powhatan's daughter . . . at most not past
13 or 14 years of age . . . oft . . . came to our fort with
what she could get [bring] for Captain Smith . . .
but her especially he ever much respected."

John Smith

⌧ ⌧ ⌧ ⌧

According to Jamestown authority Philip L. Barbour, Pocahontas was most likely born between the summers of 1595 and 1596. Her name is recognizable to anyone with any degree of interest in American history as being the savior of Captain John Smith when he was a captive of her father, Chief Powhatan. Whether or not her rescue of Smith was as colorful and flamboyant as the captain later described it in his book is another matter, but, nevertheless, the young Indian woman has survived the years as America's first heroine.

During the year, 1613, affairs in Jamestown deteriorated, primarily because of renewed Indian hostility. As a poorly devised defense, Pocahontas was captured and held hostage by the English until her father's people ceased their warring activities. Ralph Hamor, a resident of Jamestown at the time and a close friend of John Rolfe, who had advanced the colony's economy by the development of marketable tobacco, later wrote that during the young woman's stay in the village, she and Rolfe fell in love.

In time, Rolfe appealed to Governor Thomas Dale for permission to marry the maiden, despite the fact that her "education hath been rude, her manners barbarous, her generation accursed and so different . . ." Hoping for a lasting peace between the two peoples, and hopeful that a marriage between Rolfe and Pocahontas could bring this about, the governor assented. Pocahontas soon accepted Christianity and was baptized with the name, Lady Rebecca. She and Rolfe were wed in the church at Jamestown in April, 1614. The following year, Pocahontas bore a male child, whom the couple named Thomas.

During 1616, John, Pocahontas, and baby Thomas – along with several other Indians – departed Jamestown aboard Governor Dale's ship, the *Treasurer,* for a visit to England. Lady Rebecca, according to a contemporary, "did not only accustom herself to civility, but still carried herself as the daughter of a king and was accordingly respected . . ." While in London, the Rolfe family had an audience with King James I and Queen Anne. The following year, Pocahontas took ill and suddenly died and was buried at nearby Gravesend. John Rolfe returned home alone.

Marriage of Pocahontas and John Rolfe
Courtesy of The Colonial Williamsburg Foundation.

Medical Matters

"The sixth of August there died John Asbie of the bloody flux.
The ninth day died George Flowre of the swelling . . . .
The fifteenth day, there died Edward Brown and Stephen Galthorpe . . . ."

George Percy

⌗ ⌗ ⌗ ⌗

Despite John Smith's joyful declaration when he set foot on Jamestown Island in May, 1607 that "heaven and earth never agree[d] better to frame a place for man's habitation," he and his companions could hardly have picked a more unhealthy place for their future home. Officials of the Virginia Company had issued strong warnings regarding potential sites for colonization, admonishing Smith and the others to refrain from:

> plant[ing] in a low or moist place, because it will prove unhealthful. You shall judge of the good air by the people; for some part of that coast where the lands are low, have their people blear[y] eyed, and with swollen bellies and legs: but if the naturals be strong and clean made, it is a true sign of wholesome soil.

In time, Jamestown Island proved to be the exact opposite of the type of site recommended. Brackish water, mosquito-infested marshes, and intense heat and humidity soon combined to make the place unfit for European habitation. From the very beginning, the two physicians who arrived with the original party – Will Wilkinson and Thomas Wotton – had their hands full ministering to the sick and dying. Of the 105 original settlers who had arrived in May, around sixty had died before summer was over.

When Lord De La Warr arrived in 1610 to rescue the struggling colony, one of his passengers was another physician, Lawrence Bohun, or Bohune. In addition to serving as medical caretaker, Bohun was an avid student of pharmacology and he often traveled across the island in search of exotic plants that might be used to treat the many diseases that regularly visited the region. One such discovery was a tree belonging to the myrtle family, the rind of which, according to William Strachey, the settlement's secretary, "is of so great force against inveterate dysenteric fluxes of which Doctor Bohun made open experiment in many of our men laboring with such diseases and therefore wishes all such physicians . . . to make use thereof."

Beginning of American Medical Research
Courtesy of the National Park Service, Colonial National Historical Park, Jamestown Collection.

Agriculture in Early Jamestown

*"It pleased God to move the Indians to bring us corn ere
it was half ripe to refresh us and in September, they brought us
great store both of corn and bread ready made."*

John Smith

⌗ ⌗ ⌗ ⌗

Officials of the Virginia Company in London never intended for the Jamestown colonists to depend on agriculture for their livelihoods. Rather, it was clear from the start that a prudent trading policy would be established with the local Indian tribes with its success insuring that food would always be available. Although some of the craftsmen, no doubt, had practiced farming back in England, the passenger rolls of the first arrivals do not identify anyone as a professional agnculturalist. William Spence, who made his appearance nearly one year after the initial landfall, may have been the first colonist to hold that honor.

The Company had issued instructions that "you choose a seat for habitation that shall not be over burdened with woods near your town, for all the men you have shall not be able to cleanse [clear] twenty acres a year... neither must you plant in a low and moist place because it will prove unhealthful . . ." In fact, a large part of Jamestown Island was covered with forests and marshy lowlands, but the colonists' leaders wisely chose one of several large clearings upon which to build the fort.

Relations with the Indians were not always cordial, however, and the natives could not be depended upon to provide food to the colonists, as evidenced, for example, during the Starving Times. Over the years, with the arrival of farmers and agriculturalists, along with the extension of habitation outside the fort and onto the mainland, farming eventually became more important to the colony's survival. Indian corn, squash, sunflowers, pumpkins, and several varieties of peas and beans were borrowed from the natives and cultivated. As far as livestock was concerned, by 1609, when John Smith returned to England, the farmers of Jamestown possessed "six mares and a horse; five or six hundred swine; as many hens and chickens; some goats [and some sheep."

Virginia farmers became increasingly proficient at growing food crops (as well as tobacco) and raising livestock. By the middle of the seventeenth century, foodstuffs were so abundant that farmers and plantation owners up and down the James River could afford to export corn and other edibles to other English colonies primarily in New England.

Agricultural Beginnings: A Farmer of 1650
Courtesy of the National Park Service, Colonial National Historical Park, Jamestown Collection.

The Arrival of the First Slaves

"He [a Dutch sea captain] brought not any thing but 20 and odd Negroes, which the Governor [Yeardley] and [Abraham Peirsey] bought for victuals . . . . at the best and easiest rates they could."

John Rolfe

▨ ▨ ▨ ▨

Near the end of August, 1619, officials at Jamestown received word that a Dutch man-of-war had tied up at nearby Point Comfort. Aboard the ship were a few black slaves procured some weeks earlier by the Dutch in the West Indies. The ship's captain told the English that he was in short supply of food and other necessities for a long voyage home and a swap was negotiated between the two parties: food and "victualles" for several of the unfortunate Negroes.

A thin line existed in early Virginia between outright slavery, wherein the individual was actually owned by a master and had very little possibility of ever gaining his freedom, and indentured servitude, which provided for a person to work off his servant's obligation over a period of a few years and emerge "free." The few existing records from Jamestown suggest that these first black slaves were very likely treated favorably and put to work side-by-side with white indentured servants. By 1625, according to the colonial records, blacks still numbered only around twenty in the colony.

For several decades after the 1619 encounter, the slavery issue appears to have caused little concern, and it generated negligible interest in the colony. However, either through normal family growth among the original arrivals and/or the importation of additional slaves, the group's population grew significantly enough by the late 1650s to prompt the Virginia Assembly to consider slave-oriented legislation.

In March, 1660, a law was passed declaring that "in case any English servant shall run away in company with any Negroes . . . the English so running away in company with them shall serve for the time of the said Negroes' absence . . . ." Another act provided that "if any slave resists his master (or other by his master's order correcting him) and by the extremity of the correction should chance to die, that his death shall not be accounted a felony, but the master (or other person appointed by the master to punish him) be acquitted from molestation, since it cannot be presumed that premeditated malice (which alone makes murder a felony) should induce any man to destroy his own estate."

By 1670, Virginia's slave population numbered around two thousand.

The Arrival of First African-Americans at Jamestown
Courtesy of The Colonial Williamsburg Foundation.

Governmental Beginnings

*"The most convenient place we could find to sit in
was the quire [choir] of the church. . . ."*

Proceedings of the Virginia Assembly

❈ ❈ ❈ ❈

Former Deputy-governor Sir George Yeardley, knighted the previous year by King James I, returned to Virginia in April, 1619, as the new governor, replacing Deputy-governor Samuel Argall. He brought with him the Virginia Company's latest charter which, among other things, called for the creation of a formal legislature and provided for the private ownership of land.

The Virginia Assembly convened for the first time at Jamestown during summer, and the meeting was attended by burgesses from the major plantations along the James River who had been elected during the previous June. The meeting was held in the church, a twenty-by-fifty-foot timber-framed building with cedar-lined interior walls that had been built by Argall two years earlier, replacing the crude, original, makeshift church that had been hastily constructed soon after the landfall of 1607 and a second church, built in 1610 by Lord De La Warr. Two burgesses from each of the existing eleven towns and plantations appeared at the initial meeting, but the two representatives from one of the plantations were disqualified.

Many issues were discussed and resolved during the six-day gathering. In order to preserve the current friendly relations with the natives, a resolution was passed that prohibited "injury or oppression . . . by the English against the Indians whereby the present peace might be disturbed and ancient quarrels might be revived." To combat laziness among the colonists, "any man . . . found to live as an idler or renegade, though a freedman, it shall be lawful for that incorporation or plantation to which he belongeth, to appoint [assign] him [to] a [master] to serve for wages till he shows apparent signs of amendment." In the future, the Assembly ruled, "no crafty or advantageous means be suffered to be put in practice for the enticing away the tenants or servants of any particular plantation from the place where they are seated." And, with an eye on possible leaner times, a law was passed requiring every house owner to annually put aside one extra barrel of corn for himself, for each member of his family, and for and each and every servant.

The sessions held in Jamestown during this hot, humid, six-day period in 1619 signified the beginnings of democracy in America, the first efforts by elected officials whose job it would be to represent the will of the people.

The First Legislative Assembly at Jamestown
Courtesy of APVA Preservation Virginia.

The Coming of the Maidens

"These women, if they marry to the public farmers,
[are] to be transported at the charges of the Company;
If otherwise, then those that take them to wife [are] to pay
the said Company their charges of transportation . . . ."

⌗ ⌗ ⌗ ⌗

No women were present among the first Virginia colonists to make landfall on Jamestown Island in May, 1607. During the fall of the following year, however, as part of Christopher Newport's second supply mission, two ladies, "Mistresse Forest and Ann Buras her maide," arrived to bring a feminine touch to the social fabric of the infant town. Mrs. Forest was married and was supposedly joining her husband in the New World. Within two months, prospect Ann Buras (or Burrows) had become the bride of John Laydon, a carpenter. The fates of Mr. and Mrs. Forest are unknown, but Ann Buras Laydon lived till at least 1625 and during the time, gave birth to four daughters.

The practically all-male populace certainly saw a need for women at Jamestown, not only to propagate the settlement, but to perform the unpopular chores that men hated doing, such as washing. Decrying his own personal situation with respect to domestic work, colonist Thomas Nichols wrote, "I could wish women might be sent over to serve the Company for that purpose for certain years whether they marry or not," quickly adding that "For all . . . I can find . . . the multitude of women do . . . nothing but . . . devour the food of the land without doing any day's deed, whereby any benefit may arise to the Company or Country."

Jamestown was still practically womanless in 1619 when the Virginia Company initiated a program whereby it would send from England "young maids to make wives for so many of the former tenants." The minutes of the Company reflect that "it was never fitter time to send them than now." The first of the ladies, about ninety, arrived at Jamestown during the following year and were heartily welcomed by a large crowd of anxious and lonely men. Over the next several years, more shiploads of females were sent from England, bringing the ratio of women to men more into parity.

Historian Carl Bridenbaugh has written that, "The quality of life at Jamestown in the first two decades was severely limited by the absence of women and children, who as the Earl of Southampton and other worthy gentlemen . . . acknowledged, were essential in forming a colony." The importation of the "maidens" to the colony went a long way toward alleviating the societal problems caused by too many long years of monastic living among the company of gentlemen.

Location of the original painting, *Arrival of the Maidens*, is unknown.
Courtesy of the National Park Service, Colonial National Historical Park, Jamestown Collection.

The reproduction quality is substandard due to the only digital image available.

Silk Culture

"There was an assay made to make silk, & surely the worms prospered excellent well, till the master workman fell sick, during which time they were eaten with rats."

John Smith

⊞ ⊞ ⊞ ⊞

As Europe emerged from the Renaissance, silk had established itself as one of the most desirable fabrics available. The extremely expensive cloth was reserved primarily for royalty and the very wealthy since it had to be imported from the Orient. Over centuries of domestication, the worm that produced the silk thread in its cocoon had evolved into an insect that was totally dependent upon human beings to supply it with nourishment and protection from the elements. An entire industry – one supported by inexpensive labor by the elderly and children of the Far East – had grown up to support the heavy demands.

An early and continuing directive of Virginia Company officials was that the Jamestown colonists produce silk. For a brief time, the settlers believed that the product would bring them the financial success that tobacco had. The supposition was precipitated by the local abundance of mulberry trees upon which silkworms feed. "By the dwelling of the savages are some great mulberry trees, and in some parts of the country, they are found growing naturally in pretty groves," wrote John Smith.

Unfortunately, silkworms were not native to the New World and the local insects believed by the colonists to be silkworms turned out to be common caterpillars. An attempt was made at cloth production using imported stocks of the worms, but the plan faltered, no doubt hindered by the inability of the colonists to appreciate the complexity of making silk. By 1621, the failure of the colonists to successfully produce silk prompted orders from London officials forbidding "any, but the council and the heads of hundreds [plantations] to wear gold in the clothes, or to wear silk till they make it themselves." As late as 1638, despite the dismal track record, the Virginia Assembly was still urging colonists to redouble their efforts and to capitalize on the industry's potential.

In 1656, an Armenian silk grower arrived in Jamestown to supervise the failing industry. Every farmer was commanded to plant ten mulberry trees per one hundred acres. All of the effort was to no avail and silk culture in Jamestown eventually passed into oblivion.

Silk Culture
Courtesy of the National Park Service, Colonial National Historical Park, Jamestown Collection.

Native Uprising

". . . it hath pleased God for our manifold sins to lay
a most lamentable affliction upon this plantation,
by the treachery of the Indians . . . ."

The Council of Virginia

❈ ❈ ❈ ❈

When Powhatan died in 1618, he was succeeded by his half-brother, Opitchapam, who proved to be an ineffective leader. Opitchapam was soon replaced by another half-brother, Opechancanough, a strong-willed individual who lived up to the standards for his tribe set by Powhatan. Peace between the colonists and Powhatan's people had always been precarious and, by the early 1620s, relations between the two peoples once again became strained.

In March, Opechancanough launched an all-out attack on the Virginia colony, and his warriors struck plantation after plantation up and down the James River. A letter written by members of the Council to the management of the Virginia Company of London, decried the situation, declaring that the Indians:

> . . . on the 22nd of March [1622], attempted in most places, under the color of unsuspected amity, in some by surprise, to have cut us off all and to have swept us away at once throughout the whole land, had it not pleased God of his abundant mercy to prevent them in many places, for which we can never sufficiently magnify His blessed name, but yet they prevailed so far, that they have massacred in all parts above three hundred men, women, and children, and have since, not only spoiled and slain divers of our cattle and some more of our people and burned most of the houses we have forsaken, but have also enforced us to quit many of our plantations.

Governor Francis Wyatt declared martial law throughout the colony. Jamestown itself escaped the Indian attacks unscathed due to an advance warning by a friendly native. However, it was used as a gathering place for English refugees from all over the eastern seaboard, causing a sudden increase in population which severely strained food reserves.

The hostilities continued for more than a year, made worse by the visitation of the dread disease, plague, which in turn was accompanied by another famine. Finally, in April, 1623, Opechancanough declared that "blood enough had already been shed on both sides," and suggested a truce.

Indian Uprising, March 22, 1622
Courtesy of the National Park Service, Colonial National Historical Park, Jamestown Collection.

Martin's Hundred

"[They] basely and barbarously murdered, not sparing . . .
man, woman or child."

A Survivor at Wolstenholme Towne

By the time the terrible events of March, 1622 struck the Virginia colony, the region's population stood at a few over 2,200 residents, the great majority of them living on farms and plantations situated along the James River and neighboring streams. A provision in the Virginia Company's latest charter relating to private land ownership had favored this growth by allowing citizens who had been on site for three years prior to 1616 to be awarded one hundred acres of land. Those who had arrived after 1616 and who had paid their own passage received fifty acres. The post-1616 arrivals whose expenses had been borne by the Company were required to serve as tenants on Company property for a period of seven years before being qualified for free land.

John Rolfe was quick to realize the importance of the land giveaway, writing that the policy gave all recipients "great content for now knowing their own lands, [and] they strive and are prepared to build houses & to clear their grounds ready to plant, which giveth . . . great encouragement, and the greatest hope to make the Colony flourish that ever yet happened to them."

In 1618, 220 new colonists arrived in Jamestown and settled a nearby 20,000-acre tract of land called Martin's Hundred, naming their primary village Wolstenholme Towne. Peace and amity with the Indians reigned for the first several years, and local tribesmen even ". . . came unarmed into our houses . . . in some places sat down at breakfast." All this ended on March 22, 1622, when all of the farms and plantations in the region were attacked by warring Indians. Only sixty-two settlers of the new plantation survived the bloodshed and all evidence of Wolstenholme Towne was destroyed except part of the church and two houses.

In May, 1624, reacting to the many adverse reports from the beleaguered colony that continued to reach him in increasing numbers, King James I revoked the Virginia Company's charter. Thus, with a stroke of the pen, Virginia passed from a private enterprise to a royal colony. The Company's bold experiment had lasted only seventeen years.

Martin's Hundred and Wolstenholme Towne were "rediscovered" on the grounds of Carter's Grove Plantation in the 1970s and the site has undergone extensive archaeological investigation.

A Dangerous Chore
Courtesy of the National Park Service, Colonial National Historical Park, Jamestown Collection.

Expanding Jamestown

"... the fort growing since to more perfection, is now at ... about half an acre ... [and] cast into the form of a triangle...."

William Strachey

⌗ ⌗ ⌗ ⌗

Although for the first few years, the mortality rate among the early settlers at Jamestown was extremely high, replacement colonists frequently arrived with supply ships. In 1616, John Rolfe estimated that the entire Virginia colony contained 351 people, including officers, laborers, workmen, women and children. By 1620, however, the population of Jamestown and its associated plantations numbered around 2,200. Although this increase does not represent a boom by any means, it does appear logical to assume that in time, the small palisaded fort could no longer hold even a modest increase of new arrivals.

Archaeological evidence suggests that by around 1615, possibly a few years before, expansion did, indeed, occur eastward to the open spaces outside the fort walls. The new development was called "New Towne" and it eventually consisted of several dwellings, service buildings, and, in time, the church and one or more statehouses.

By the mid-1620s, New Towne was a thriving place bustling with activities. A flurry of land grants bestowed to both established and newly arrived settlers fueled the economy. Evidence of the rapid growth of the area can be ascertained in the text of the following land grant decree to Ralph Hamor.

> I, Sir Francis Wyatt, knight governor and captain general of Virginia do with the consent of the Council of State give and grant unto Ralph Hamor, Esq. and one of the said Council of State and to his heirs and assigns forever for the better convenience and more commodity of his houses by him erected and built in the New Towne within the precincts of James City one acre and a half of ground lying and being about his said house and abutting southward upon the highway along the bank of the main river, northward upon the back street, eastward upon the highway which parts it from the ground of George Menefey, merchant, westward partly upon the ground of Richard Stephens, merchant, and upon the ground, also of John Chew, merchant, the said ground of one acre and a half partly belonging unto his aforesaid house already built & partly unto a house hereafter to be built by him ....

Jamestown About 1619
Courtesy of the National Park Service, Colonial National Historical Park, Jamestown Collection.

Prosperity at New Towne

*". . . [outside] this town in the Island are some very pleasant
and beautiful houses, two blockhouses to observe and watch least
the Indians at any time should swim over the back river
and come into the island, and certain other farm houses."*

Ralph Hamor

Following the Indian uprising of 1622, the continuing development of the tobacco economy went a long way in allowing Jamestown to prosper, particularly considering the spiraling profitability of the plant in England and on the Continent. New Towne became the abode of a rising number of skilled craftsmen, as well as prominent "first settlers" and government officials. A little earlier, Ralph Hamor described the rapidly growing village.

> Jamestown [is] situated upon a goodly and fertile island which although formerly scandalized with unhealthful air, we have since approved as healthful as any other place in the country; and this I can say by my own experience, that the corn and garden ground (which with much labor being when we first seated upon it, a thick woods) we have cleared and impaled, is as fertile as any other we have had experience and trial of. The town itself . . . is reduced into a handsome form and hath in it two fair rows of houses, all of framed timber, two stories [high], and an upper garret, or corn loft . . . besides three large and substantial storehouses, joined together in length some hundred and twenty foot, and in breadth forty, and this town hath been lately newly and strongly impaled and a fair platform for ordnance in the west bulwark raised . . . .

In 1634, as prosperity at last came to the residents of Jamestown, Virginia officials divided the colony into eight "shires" or counties, civic designations that had already been a part of England's heritage for many years: James City, Henrico, Charles City, Elizabeth City, Warrascoyack (changed to Isle of Wight in 1637), Charles River, Warwick River, and Accomac (spelled without a "k"). The office of sheriff, the shire's highest ranking government official, was also created. The 2,500 residents who called Virginia home in 1630 increased dramatically over the next decade to more than ten thousand, populating the nearly one hundred towns, villages, and plantations scattered along the James, York, and Rappahannock Rivers.

Marketplace at Jamestown
Courtesy of the Jamestown-Yorktown Foundation.

Brick Making

"It is quite clear from documentary records and archaeological remains, that the colonists not only made their own brick, but that the process, as well as the finished products, followed closely the English method."

J. Paul Hudson

▦ ▦ ▦ ▦

Although two bricklayers and a mason were among the original 105 colonists to arrive at Jamestown in 1607, no houses built completely with bricks appear to have been completed in the region until the late 1630s. Over the years, however, several brick kilns have been unearthed, suggesting that bricks were in common use, even though not for houses. Archaeological findings indicate that the craftsmen were kept busy during the early years laying bricks for the foundations of frame houses, water well linings, fireboxes, and chimneys.

Brick making was a rather complex business and, although no contemporary accounts exist describing the procedures used at Jamestown, an ancient document from England dating to the same period outlines the basic tenets of brick manufacture as, no doubt, practiced in the colony. It reads:

1. Before Christmas we begin to dig the earth and let it lie to mellow till Easter.
2. Then we water the earth well and temper it with a narrow spade.
3. The moulder cuts off a piece of earth, throws it into the mould made of beech, leveling it off with a wooden implement called a strike.
4. The carrier carries the mould to the drying ground, where he adroitly turns it over, laying the bricks on the ground, and lifts up the mould.
5. When the bricks are dry, they carry them to a place where they row them up like a wall. They are covered with straw, till they are dry enough to be carried to the kiln.
6. Then they are stacked in the kiln, a fire kept till they are at the top red fire hot.
7. Then we let them cool, and sell them as we can for as much money as we can get, but usually about 13 or 14 shillings the thousand.

The Brickmaker: Brick Making
Courtesy of the National Park Service, Colonial National Historical Park, Jamestown Collection.

The First Brick House

*"There are twelve houses and stores built in the Towne,
one of brick by the Secretary, the fairest that ever was known
in this country for substance and uniformity. . . ."*

Governor John Harvey

⊠ ⊠ ⊠ ⊠

When English colonists first landed on Jamestown Island in 1607, one of the first problems they faced was the building of houses for protection from the elements and the potential hostility of neighboring Indians. Past and present archaeological studies have pretty much proven that the first houses on the Island were made of sticks and mud, sometimes called "wattle and daub." This type of housing was probably soon followed by the use of frame materials. In both instances, the roofs were covered with grass and reeds, much as the traditional residences in England were. One story cabins were eventually superceded by rather substantial two-story affairs, similar to the ones described by Ralph Hamor as being "of framed timber, two stories, and an upper garret . . . ."

Only after the late 1630s did brick houses appear with any consistency. In 1957, J. Paul Hudson, curator of the Jamestown Museum, whose historical studies in many cases provided the scientific "proof" upon which many of Sidney King's paintings were based, described the evolution of house-building at Jamestown when he wrote:

> Timber at Jamestown was plentiful, so many houses, especially in the early years, were of frame construction. During the first decade or two, house construction reflected a primitive use found ready at hand, such as saplings for a sort of framing, and use of branches, leafage, bark, and animal skins. During these early years – when the settlers were having such a difficult time staying alive – mud walls, wattle and daub, and coarse marshgrass thatch were used. Out of these years of improvising, construction with squared posts, and later with quarterings (studs), came into practice. There was little thought of plastering walls during the first two decades, and when plastering was adopted, clay, or clay mixed with oyster-shell lime, was first used. The early floors were of clay, and such floors continued to be used in the humbler dwellings throughout the 1600s. . . . After Jamestown had attained some degree of permanency, many houses were built of brick.

Jamestown: Typical Brick Residence
Courtesy of the National Park Service, Colonial National Historical Park, Jamestown Collection.

Legislative Matters

"[Authorize] at ye public charge of ye country a convenient house to
be built where you and the council may meet and sit for dispatching
of public affairs and hearing causes."

Sir William Berkeley

⊠ ⊠ ⊠ ⊠

For exactly how long the Jamestown church served as the colony's statehouse, wherein official governmental business was transacted, is uncertain. However, based on the latest archaeological findings unearthed by the Jamestown Rediscovery project, it might have been utilized until the late 1620s or early 1630s, at which time, the Assembly moved its meeting place to Sir (Governor) John Harvey's residence located in the "New Town" section of the village.

In July, 1621, while apparently still operating out of the church, it was determined "by authority directed . . . from His Majesty under his Great Seal," that two separate councils would be established to improve government in the colony. The "Council of State" was to consist of individuals selected by the Virginia Company, while the "General Assembly" was to be filled with two burgesses from each of the plantations and towns in the colony.

Three years later, King James I revoked the Virginia Company's charter, effectively taking Virginia out of private ownership and giving it crown colony status. The following year, in April, a new council, operating under the authority of the Crown, met at Jamestown. Francis Wyatt, who had served as governor for the Virginia Company since 1621, was kept in office under the new regime. The council consisted of Francis West, George Yeardley, George Sandys, Roger Smyth, Ralph Hamor, John Martin, John Harvey, Samuel Mathews, Abraham Peirsey, Isaac Maddison, and William Claiborne.

In 1630, John Harvey became governor and, although unpopular with the people, he managed to hold his job for the next five years. It was apparently soon after his appointment that his private residence became Virginia's statehouse for the next fifteen years, at least in part, since evidence suggests that during some of this time, the Council met there, while the House of Burgesses convened in another building known as "the country's house."

William Berkeley became Virginia's governor in 1642 and immediately set about to have his residence built. The resulting house, Berkeley's Row, also saw duty as the new statehouse until around 1665, when the seat of government once again moved, this time to a structure built specifically for its use and occupancy.

Second Statehouse and Outbuildings
Courtesy of the National Park Service, Colonial National Historical Park, Jamestown Collection.

Barrel Making

"It's fair to guess that in the South there were more coopers than any other kind of artisan."

Edwin Tunis

⊠ ⊠ ⊠ ⊠

The importance of the cooper, or barrel maker, in early Virginia cannot be overestimated. Literally anything that had to be stored or transported had to be put in a barrel – tobacco, indigo, flour and meal, sassafras, tar, meat, and salt, to name a few items.

The first cooper in Jamestown was John Lewes, who arrived in 1608 aboard the first re-supply ship. Others of the trade soon followed. An early book on tradesmen described the typical cooper's duties:

> A cooper manufactures casks, tubs of all sizes, pails, and sundry other articles useful in domestic concerns. These are made with oak timber . . . cut up into narrow pieces called staves; they are sometimes bent, and for other sorts of work they are straight. For tubs, pails, &c. the bottoms of which are less than the tops, the staves are wider at top than they are at the bottom. These staves are kept together by means of hoops, which are made of hazel and ash; but some articles require iron hoops. To make them hold water or other liquids, the cooper places between each stave from top to bottom split flags, which swell with moisture, and . . . prevent the vessel from leaking.

The cooper utilized several varieties of special tools, among them the adz, a specialized form of axe, with which he separated staves from the main source of wood; the spoke-shave, or draw-knife, which was used to shave off excess wood and smooth the staves; the stock-and-bit, more commonly called a brace-and-bit, to drill holes; and augers for boring larger holes into the wood. Continuing, the above reference declares that the:

> cooper carries with him a few hoops of different sizes, some iron rivets, and wooden pegs, his hammer, adze, and stock-and-bit. With these few instruments he can repair all washing and brewing utensils, besides the churns and wooden vessels made use of dairies. An ingenious working cooper will in his peregrinations readily perform sundry jobs that belong to the carpenter."

The Cooper at Work
Courtesy of the National Park Service, Colonial National Historical Park, Jamestown Collection.

Wine Making

"There grow in that country [Virginia] wild many forest grapes,
of which the English make a wine that resembles much the wine
of Alicante, according to the opinion of the narrator who has tasted both."

Francisco Maguel

✦ ✦ ✦ ✦

Wild grape vines were among the first plants discovered on Jamestown Island in 1607 when the colonists arrived. Probably a variant of today's scuppernong grape, the fruit, though plentiful, did not lend itself to the manufacture of good wine. The quality of the beverage was further compromised when the vintners attempted to ship it to England; the long overseas journey was just too much for the delicacy and, in a high percentage of cases, it spoiled long before it reached its European destination.

Nevertheless, a dozen years after first settlement, Jamestown entrepreneurs were still attempting to make a profitable business out of wine making. That year a law was passed requiring every householder to plant at least ten grape vines annually to further the wine industry on the island. This attempt led nowhere and, in time, wine making, other than for personal consumption, more or less disappeared from the region.

In the year 1685, a book published in London described the wine making process that was very likely identical to the manner in which the industry was pursued in early Jamestown when it appeared that the industry would turn into a profitable endeavor.

> Wine groweth in the vineyard, where vines are propagated and tied with twigs to trees or to props or frames. When the time of grape gathering is come, they cut off the bunches and carry them in measures of three bushels and throw them into a vat and tread them with their feet or tramp them with a wooden pestle and squeeze out the juice in the wine-press which is called must and being received in a great tub, it is poured into hogsheads. It is stopped up and, being laid close in cellars upon settling, it becometh wine. It is drawn out of the hogshead with a cock, or faucet . . . .

Thousands of wine bottles and other glass and ceramic ware associated with wine have been unearthed at Jamestown, suggesting that, although of poor quality and unprofitable, wine was, nevertheless, a popular beverage of the times.

Wine Making – a 17th Century Enterprise

Courtesy of the National Park Service, Colonial National Historical Park, Jamestown Collection.

Pottery

"The Jamestown potter, indeed, was no young apprentice or mere farmer who potted on the side. The potter's art, then as now, was a highly specialized one, rooted in a long tradition. Our potter was an artisan, trained in the mysteries of a medieval craft, and it was probably he who first transplanted his ancient skills to the Virginia wilderness."

J. Paul Hudson

❖ ❖ ❖ ❖

Since serious archaeological investigation began at Jamestown almost one hundred years ago, remains of the potter's art have probably contributed more than any other evidence to a proper understanding of life in the colonial town. During the decade (1994-2004) encompassing the Jamestown Rediscovery Project, several hundred thousand artifacts have been unearthed on the island, a large proportion of them having to do with ceramics.

Many types of pottery, each requiring special skills, were manufactured in early Virginia. Not only common earthenware, but more sophisticated forms of slip-decorated and lead-glazed ware were made, while other varieties, including English delftware, German salt-glazed stoneware, and Italian and Spanish majolica were imported from Europe.

The unnamed writer of an old book on ancient crafts and trades described the potter's art and the common tools of the trade when he wrote:

> The wheel and the lathe are the chief instruments in the business of pottery: the first is intended for large works, and the other for small; the wheel is turned by a labourer . . . but the lathe is put into motion by the foot of the workman. When the clay is properly prepared, and made into lumps proportioned to the size of a cup, plate, or other vessel to be made, the potter places one of these lumps upon the head of the wheel before him, which he turns round, while he forms the cavity of the vessel with his finger and thumb, continuing to widen it from the middle, and thus turning the inside into form with one hand, while he proportions the outside with the other, the wheel being kept the whole time in constant motion. The mouldings are formed by holding a piece of wood or iron, cut into the shape of the moulding, to the vessel while the wheel is going round; but the feet and handles are made by themselves, and set on by the hand . . . .

Making Pottery at Jamestown
Courtesy of the National Park Service, Colonial National Historical Park, Jamestown Collection.

Making Potash

*". . . we can by our industry . . . make oils, wines, soap ashes,
wood ashes, extract from mineral earth, iron, copper &c. . . ."*

Gabriel Archer

※ ※ ※ ※

Potash and soap ashes were used in both Europe and the New World for soap and glass making. In fact, the two commodities were among the first imports that Virginians shipped back to England. The abundant forests from which these products were derived made their manufacture relatively easy, and they proved to be extremely profitable for the otherwise struggling colony. Within two years of the initial landing, Peter Wynne, who had admitted that "I was not so desirous to come into this country, as I am now willing here to end my days," wrote to a friend in England that resources were abundant in the colony and that many were to be had in "great store, [among them] pitch, tar, soap ashes, and some dyes, whereof we have sent examples."

In his book, *A Map of Virginia,* John Smith referred to the soap ash industry when he wrote, "There is also some elm, some black walnut trees, and some ash: of ash and elm they make soap ashes. If the trees be very great, the ashes will be good and melt to hard lumps, but if they be small, it will be but powder and not so good as the other."

The Jamestown historian, J. Paul Hudson, has written that the manufacture of potash and soap ashes required five basic steps, summarized below:

1. A stack of hardwood – preferably beech, hazel nut, ash, oak, elm, hickory, or tulip poplar – was gathered and set ablaze. The pile was allowed to burn until its ashes turned gray in color.
2. When several pounds of ashes were ready, they were leached in a large receptacle by mixing them with boiling water.
3. The residual, called lye, was strained through cloth to separate foreign objects from the liquid.
4. The remaining liquid was placed in a large iron pot and allowed to evaporate over an open flame.
5. The residue in the bottom of the pot was placed in another pot and allowed to melt. When the resultant semi-liquid was poured onto an iron plate and allowed to cool, it transformed into potash.

Potash and Soap Ash Production
Courtesy of the National Park Service, Colonial National Historical Park, Jamestown Collection.

Harvesting Ice

*"An extremely important discovery was a large, deep, ice-storage pit,
believed to be the only 17th century ice pit which has been
excavated [as of 1957 when this was written] in Virginia."*

John L. Cotter
J. Paul Hudson

⊠ ⊠ ⊠ ⊠

In order to resolve the problem of storing perishable food and preserving ice as long as possible into warm weather, Jamestown residents resorted to a device that most of them were already familiar with from their years in the Old Country. The ice storage pit, basically a simple ice house, was dug deep into the ground and covered with a fourteen-foot, circular, brick structure that most likely stood about ten feet above the ground. Such a pit was discovered by archaeologists in the mid-1950s and it stood around 250 feet east of the former Visitor Center.

The early ice house served much the same purpose as the later cellar did: a place for storage of perishable goods. In fact, Eric Sloane, the noted author and illustrator of numerous books on early America, has written that the word, cellar, derives from the French word, *cella,* meaning store-room. He explains that the depth of the underground part of the room was far enough below ground to maintain a cool temperature in the summer, yet was not so deep that the temperature reached freezing in the winter.

The ice house made it possible for milk, cheese, meat, vegetables, fish, and other perishables to have their useful lives extended by many weeks. And, as its name suggests, it was also utilized for the storage of ice which was cut from nearby ponds during freezing weather. The 1600s witnessed a protracted, severe drought along the entire Atlantic coast of North America, but the winters during the same period, part of the so-called "Little Ice Age," were so frigid that parts of the Chesapeake Bay froze over during both the winters of 1641-42 and 1645-46. The winter of 1697-98 has been termed one of the worst ever to visit the New World. So, although Jamestown's normally hot and humid summertime weather severely restricted the preservation of perishable goods, the ice pit and ice house went a long way toward preserving commodities that otherwise would be useless without some form of refrigeration.

Storing Ice: Ice Harvesting
Courtesy of the National Park Service, Colonial National Historical Park, Jamestown Collection.

The Continued Popularity of Tobacco

"And surely, in my opinion, there cannot be a more base, and yet hurtful, corruption in a country, than is the vile use . . . of . . . tobacco . . . ."

King James I

❖ ❖ ❖ ❖

In 1625, at the age of fifty-nine, England's King James I went to his grave still despising tobacco, which by then had become the mainstay export of his namesake outpost in the New World, Jamestown. Early in his reign, he had published a pamphlet entitled, *A Counterblaste to Tobacco,* in which he harshly criticized the tobacco habit and demonstrated an amazingly modern understanding of the harm it could bring.

> Have you not reason to be ashamed, and to forbear this filthy novelty, so basely grounded, so foolishly received, and so grossly mistaken in the right use thereof? In your abuse thereof sinning against God, harming yourselves both in persons and goods, and making also thereby the marks and notes of vanity upon you . . . . [It is] a custom loathsome to the eye, hateful to the nose, harmful to the brain, dangerous to the lungs, and in the black, stinking fume thereof, nearest resembling the horrible Stygian smoke of the pit that is bottomless.

The admonitions of King James, like those of the U. S. Surgeon General three hundred and fifty years later, fell on deaf ears. By the time of his demise, use of tobacco in England and the rest of Europe was both popular and commonplace, and the demand for fine quality tobacco was constant. In 1619, John Pory, a Jamestown resident, declared, "All our riches for the present do consist of tobacco, wherein one man by his own labor, hath in one year raised to himself . . . the value of 200£." Four years later, a local official admitted that ". . . there is no commodity but tobacco." And, in 1626, the colony's governor even lamented "that nothing hath hindered the proceedings of . . . trades and staple commodities more than the want of money amongst us; which makes all men apply themselves to tobacco . . . . (which is our money) . . . ."

By 1640, the Virginia colony's population had grown to more than ten thousand, including many farmers and plantation owners whose number one cash crop was tobacco. The following year, 1,300,000 pounds of the plant were exported at an average price of two pence per pound.

A Shipping Scene
Courtesy of the National Park Service, Colonial National Historical Park, Jamestown Collection.

Shipbuilding in Jamestown and Vicinity

"A ship has been defined [as] a timber building, consisting of various parts and pieces, nailed and pinned together with iron and wood, in such form as to be fit to float, and to be conducted by wind and sails from sea to sea."

The Book of Trades, or Library of the Useful Arts

⬚ ⬚ ⬚ ⬚

Of all the natural resources that the Jamestown colonists discovered as they explored the newfound lands of Virginia, the one that impressed them most was the vast forests containing tall, straight timber. Coming from a country like England where deep woods and forests were rare, the adventurers immediately recognized that they had settled in a shipbuilder's paradise. "Oaks there are as fair, straight and tall and as good timber as any can be found, a great store, in some places very great," declared one observer, adding that "Walnut trees were many, excellent fair timber above four-score foot, straight without a bough." Another declared, "We shall fell our timber, saw our planks, and quickly make good shipping there, and shall return, thence with good employment, an hundred sail of ships yearly."

For some time after the site of Jamestown was settled in 1607, the nucleus of the English population centered there. Eventually, bold settlers opened up new lands beyond the fort and, by the time of the great Indian massacre in 1622, several plantations ranged up and down the James River and beyond. Most of these holdings maintained their own ship building facilities where several varieties of sea-going craft were built.

In 1662, the Assembly passed legislation specifically designed to accommodate boat and ship builders, declaring that "every one that shall build a small vessel with a deck be allowed, if above twenty and under fifty tons, fifty pounds of tobacco per ton; if above fifty and under one hundred tons, one hundred pounds of tobacco per ton; if above one hundred tons, two hundred pounds per ton . . . . Provided the vessel is not sold except to an inhabitant of this country in three years."

Eighteen years later, the body enacted a law that designated certain communities to serve as official "trading towns," to which farmers and plantation owners could conveniently carry their produce, especially tobacco, for export. Among the villages established at the time – all of which had their own shipyards – were Henrico, Surry, James City, Elizabeth City, York, Gloucester, and Lancaster.

Boat Building at Jamestown
Courtesy of the National Park Service, Colonial National Historical Park, Jamestown Collection.

Bacon's Rebellion

"Of these the aforesaid articles we accuse Sir William Berkeley as guilty of each and every one of the same, and as one who hath traitorously attempted, violated, and injured his Majesty's interest here . . . ."

Nathaniel Bacon, Junior

⊠ ⊠ ⊠ ⊠

In September, 1676, during a short-lived rebellion, the Virginia colony's primary town at Jamestown was destroyed by fire. The culprits were followers of Nathaniel Bacon, Jr., a young backwoodsman who had repeatedly petitioned the governor, William Berkeley, for redress on several matters, among them, protection from the Indians. Bacon, twenty-seven years old and Cambridge-educated, was a cousin by marriage to the governor. He had arrived in Virginia two years earlier, purchasing a large tobacco plantation and accepting a seat on the Council.

Berkeley steadfastly refused aid to Bacon and his neighbors and, earlier in the year, Bacon had taken matters into his own hands and massacred a number of Occaneechi Indians, even though the tribe was friendly to the Virginia settlers. When the governor refused to sign a commission making Bacon the commander-in-chief, an honor already bestowed upon him by the Assembly, Bacon torched Jamestown. A contemporary account of the incident relates that:

> Bacon enters it [Jamestown] without any opposition and . . . instantly resolves to lay it level with the ground, and the same night he became possessed of it, set fire to [the] town, church, and state house wherein were the country's records . . . .

Later in the year, Bacon succumbed to "lice and flux" and the revolt soon died as well, causing Berkeley to order a series of ruthless reprisals that lasted into the following year. Among those executed for their participation in the uprising were Thomas Young, Henry Page, Thomas Hall, William Drummond, John Baptista, James Crews, William Cookson, John Digbie, Giles Bland, Anthony Arnold, John Isles, Richard Pomfrey, John Whitson, and William Scarburgh, all hanged between January and March, 1677.

Following the carnage of Bacon's Rebellion and its bloody aftermath, Berkeley was ordered by King Charles II to return to England. He was an ill man when he departed Jamestown in April, dying three months later.

Bacon's Rebellion, 1676
Courtesy of the National Park Service, Colonial National Historical Park, Jamestown Collection.

The Final Statehouses

". . . the charge the country is yearly at for houses for
the quarter courts and assemblys to sit in would in
two or 3 years defray the purchase of a state house."

Minutes from the House of Burgesses.

⊠ ⊠ ⊠ ⊠

By 1665, the Virginia government was operating out of its fifth home, a long, brick row house situated near the James River west of the original fort. For the first time, burgesses deliberated in a structure that served as a permanent base, rather than suffering "the dishonour of all our laws being made and our judgments given in alehouses." Initially, the building housed the jail and, eventually, several of its units were leased to prominent residents. But, by and large, it was used for governmental functions and that is the role it played until it burned to the ground during Bacon's Rebellion in 1676.

For nearly a decade, between 1676 and 1685, when the final statehouse was completed, the Council and House of Burgesses met elsewhere. One location was Green Spring, the palatial home of Governor William Berkeley located three miles west of Jamestown, whence the governor orchestrated his reign of terror against Bacon's followers. Other rendezvous included the homes and/or ordinaries of Mrs. Ann Macon, William Sherwood, Henry Gawler, and Captain William Armiger.

A notation by the Council dated October 5, 1685, reveals that ". . . in order to hold a General Assembly . . . they [the burgesses] repair[ed] to the . . . state house," indicating that the final statehouse to be built in Jamestown was ready for occupancy. It rose from the foundations of the previous structure and conformed very closely to the design of the burned out edifice. According to Dr. William M. Kelso, the leader of the Jamestown Rediscovery project,

> . . . the 1665-1698 State House complex in its day was the largest secular public building in 17th century America. With its two stories and garrets, additions, porch chambers, cellars and a stair tower, the complex totaled 23,000 square feet under one roof. No other governmental/public building in Colonial America was even close to that scale.

On October 20, 1698, the final statehouse met the same fate as its predecessor, burning to the ground, possibly the result of a jail inmate's intentional fire. The building's destruction was instrumental in the decision the following year to move Virginia's capital from Jamestown to Middle Plantation (Williamsburg).

The Third State House
Courtesy of APVA Preservation Virginia.

The End of an Era

"The committee having maturely considered . . . the matters . . .
relating to the place for erecting and building a state house
after the nomination of several places . . . . resolved that
the said state house be built at the Middle Plantation."

Journals of the House of Burgesses

⌗ ⌗ ⌗ ⌗

For ninety-two years from its founding in 1607, Jamestown remained Virginia's capital. During its early days, it had been threatened with failure by starvation, the elements, disease, fire, hostile Indians, inept governors, and lackadaisical management. Yet it had survived for nearly a century as the colony's most important settlement and, in doing so, it had provided home-sweet-home to hundreds, and eventually thousands, of hardworking, faceless individuals who never knew that their endeavors would go down in the history books as the first permanent English colonization in North America. They had literally created their paradise on earth out of a ruthless, unforgiving wilderness, yet rose above all adversities to thrive.

There were times when the town's future was in doubt. During the early 1660s, rather than abandoning the site for a more practical and convenient location, the Assembly gave its vote of confidence by passing legislation that would breathe new life into Jamestown. The enabling act called for "a town be built at James City as being the most convenient place in James River and already best fitted for the entertainment of workmen that must be employed in the work." Houses were to be built entirely of brick, with no new frame structures permitted. Existing frame buildings were not to be repaired, but replaced by brick ones.

In 1698, a disastrous fire destroyed the statehouse, presenting an opportunity for the Assembly to consider another site as the colony's capital. By then, Jamestown contained about thirty houses and several hundred residents, and Governor Francis Nicholson was complaining that the town was "reduced to so mean a condition that it cannot give entertainment to people attending both a General Assembly and a General Court together." In May, 1699, the Assembly voted to relocate Virginia's capital and seat of governmental functions to Middle Plantation, thus ringing the death knell for Jamestown.

In 1703, somewhat belatedly, Queen Anne notified Virginia officials that her desire was to maintain the capital at Jamestown. It was too late; construction on the new capitol building had already begun as Williamsburg entered into its own long and illustrious history.

A Family at Home, 1650
Courtesy of the National Park Service, Colonial National Historical Park, Jamestown Collection.

Rediscovering Jamestown

". . . the first fort site of 1607, of which no trace has been found on land, is thought to have been eaten away, together with the old powder magazine and much early 17th-century property fronting on the river."

John L. Cotter and J. Paul Hudson

⌘ ⌘ ⌘ ⌘

Until the 1990s, the above quotation pretty well summed up the consensus among historians and archaeologists about the fate of James Fort. Written by two authorities on early Jamestown and published in a National Park Service booklet that appeared in 1957, just in time for the 350th celebration of the original settlement of Virginia, the attitude was based on years of on-again, off-again archaeological exploration on Jamestown Island that had failed to yield any clues relative to the exact location of the elusive fort.

Preservation activities on the island began in 1893 when The Association for the Preservation of Virginia Antiquities (APVA) purchased 22.5 acres of the original town site, centered around the old church. A decade later, the organization was instrumental in persuading the U. S. Army Corps of Engineers to build a protective wall that lined the bank of the James River along the site, thus preventing erosion from destroying any more of the former village.

In 1994, the APVA organized an extensive, multi-disciplinary effort called Jamestown Rediscovery, among the goals of which was to locate the original 1607 fort and to analyze and publish its secrets in time for the 400th Anniversary Celebration in 2007. Dr. William Kelso and a team of scientists began work immediately and, during the 1994 digging season, uncovered 30,000 objects, many of them dating from the first settlement period. Even more exciting, Kelso and his associates found evidence of the much sought-after fort, thus projecting the theory that the palisaded structure might not have been lost to the hungry waters of the James River after all.

As work progressed over the next decade, Kelso and his dedicated staff pursued their goals every summer and, despite such natural maladies as the destructive forces of Hurricane Isabel, added many hundreds of thousands more artifacts to the assemblage. More importantly, they proved, once and for all, that the vast majority of the original, triangular-shaped fort's footprint still exists on the bank of the James. Only one of the three bastions and a small length of palisades appear to have been lost to the river.

Indians Watching the Colonists Construct the James Fort, May 1607
Courtesy of the National Park Service, Colonial National Historical Park, Jamestown Collection.

Bibliography

Barbour, Philip L., editor. *The Jamestown Voyages under the First Charter 1606-1609.* Two volumes. Cambridge: Cambridge University Press for the Hakluyt Society, 1969.

Blanton, Wyndham B. *Medicine in Virginia in the Seventeenth Century.* Richmond: The William Byrd Press, Inc., 1930.

Bridenbaugh, Carl. *Jamestown 1544-1699.* New York: Oxford University Press, 1980.

Carrier, Lyman. *Agriculture in Virginia, 1607-1699.* Williamsburg: Virginia 350th Anniversary Celebration Corporation, 1957.

Cotter, John L. and J. Paul Hudson. *New Discoveries at Jamestown.* Washington, D. C.: U. S. Government Printing Office, 1957.

Crutchfield, James A. *A Primer of Handicrafts of the Southern Appalachians.* Nashville: Williams Press, 1976.

————————————————. *The Grand Adventure: A Year by Year History of Virginia.* Richmond: The Dietz Press, 2005.

Fagan, Brian. *The Little Ice Age: How Climate Made History 1300-1850.* New York: Basic Books, 2000.

Hatch, Charles E., Jr. *America's Oldest Legislative Assembly & Its Jamestown Statehouses.* Washington, D. C.: U. S. National Park Service, 1956.

Herndon, Melvin. *Tobacco in Colonial Virginia: "The Sovereign Remedy."* Williamsburg: Virginia 350th Anniversary Celebration Corporation, 1957.

Hudson, J. Paul, with illustrations by Sidney King. "Augustine Washington," in *The Iron Worker.* Volume XXV, No. 3. Lynchburg: Lynchburg Foundry Company, 1961.

————————. "America's History Visualized Through Paintings," in *The Iron Worker*. Volume XXVI, No. 1. Lynchburg: Lynchburg Foundry Company, 1962.

Hughes, Thomas P. *Medicine in Virginia, 1607-1699*. Williamsburg: Virginia 350th Anniversary Celebration Corporation, 1957.

————————. *The Virginia Adventure*. New York: Alfred A. Knopf, 1998.

Kelso, William M. with Beverly Straube. *Jamestown Rediscovery: 1994-2004*. Richmond: The Association for the Preservation of Virginia Antiquities, 2004.

Kelso, William M., et al. *Rediscovering Jamestown: The Search for the 1607 James Fort*. Seven volumes. Richmond: The Association for the Preservation of Virginia Antiquities, 1995-2001.

King, Sidney E. and J. Paul Hudson. *A Pictorial Album of Jamestown*. NP, 1963.

McCartney, Martha W. *Jamestown: An American Legacy*. NP: Eastern National, 2001.

Noël Hume, Ivor. *Martin's Hundred*. New York: Alfred A. Knopf, 1982.

Riley, Edward M. and Charles E. Hatch, Jr., editors. *James Towne in the Words of Contemporaries*. Washington D. C.: National Park Service Source Book Series No. 5, 1955.

Stockham, Peter, editor. *Little Book of Early American Crafts & Trades*. New York: Dover Publications, Inc., 1976.

Swanton, John R. *The Indian Tribes of North America*. Bureau of American Ethnology Bulletin Number 145. Washington D. C.: U. S. Printing Office for the Smithsonian Institution, 1952.

The Annals of America, Volume 1, 1493-1754, Discovering a New World. Chicago: Encyclopaedia Britannica, Inc., 1968.

Tunis, Edwin. *Colonial Craftsmen*. New York: Thomas Y. Crowell Co., 1965.

————————. *Colonial Living*. Cleveland: The World Publishing Company, 1957.

Waldman, Carl. *Atlas of the North American Indian*. New York: Facts on File Publications, 1985.